40 Days to H

Holistic Health

Welcome to "40 Days to Holistic Health: A Spiritual Journey for Body, Mind, and Soul." Over the next **40 days**, we will embark on a transformative journey toward better health and spiritual growth.

Holistic health recognizes the interconnectedness of our physical, mental, emotional, and spiritual well-being. By addressing each of these aspects, we can work towards achieving balance and harmony in our lives.

In our fast-paced, modern world, we often overlook the importance of nurturing our body, mind, and soul.

We become consumed by the demands of daily life, and our well-being suffers as a result. It is crucial to remember that our health is not solely determined by our physical condition but also by our emotional and spiritual state.

This book is designed to help you explore and improve all aspects of your health over the course of **40 days.** Each day, you will be presented with a reflection, a Bible passage, an application, and a prayer.

These elements will guide you through various topics related to holistic health and spiritual growth. By the end of this journey, you will have a deeper understanding of your body, mind, and soul, and will be equipped with the tools to nurture them.

Our spiritual lives directly influence our overall well-being. When our spiritual health suffers, it can manifest as physical or emotional ailments. On the other hand, a strong spiritual foundation can promote healing and resilience in the face of life's challenges.

Throughout this journey, we will look to the Bible for guidance, wisdom, and encouragement. The Scriptures provide a roadmap for living a healthy, balanced life, and can serve as a source of hope and inspiration during difficult times.

This journey is not about achieving perfection, but rather about cultivating awareness, making conscious choices, and taking small steps toward holistic health. Each day, you will be encouraged to examine your habits, beliefs, and thought patterns and consider how they may be impacting your well-being.

You will be challenged to make positive changes, develop healthier habits, and deepen your spiritual connection with God.

As you progress through the **40 days,** it is essential to practice self-compassion and patience. Holistic health is a lifelong pursuit, and this journey is just the beginning. Use this time to establish a strong foundation for lasting change, but remember that growth and healing take time. Trust in the process, and celebrate your progress along the way.

In the pages that follow, you will find guidance, inspiration, and support for your journey toward holistic health. It is our hope that these daily devotionals will serve as a valuable resource and a source of encouragement as you take steps to nurture your body, mind, and soul.

We invite you to join us on this transformative journey, and we pray that it will lead you to a deeper connection with God and a greater sense of well-being and fulfillment.

Let us begin our journey to holistic health and spiritual growth together, as we seek to honor our bodies as temples of the Holy Spirit, renew our minds, and nurture our souls.

May this 40-day journey be a time of reflection, growth, and healing as we strive to live abundantly and wholeheartedly, in accordance with God's design for our lives.

Day 1: The Foundation of Holistic Health

Reflection

Holistic health is a journey that encompasses the well-being of your body, mind, and soul. It is a lifestyle that prioritizes balance, self-care, and personal growth, with an emphasis on the interconnectedness of all aspects of your life.

As you begin this 40-day journey, take a moment to reflect on your current state of health and well-being, and consider how a holistic approach might help you achieve greater balance, vitality, and fulfillment.

Bible Passage : 1 Corinthians 6:19-20 (NIV)

Do you not know that your bodies are temples of the Holy Spirit, who is in you, whom you have received from God? You are not your own; you were bought at a price.

Therefore, honor God with your bodies.

Bible Passage : 3 John 1:2 (NIV)

Dear friend, I pray that you may enjoy good health and that all may go well with you, even as your soul is getting along well.

Application

Take some time to assess your current state of health in the areas of physical, mental, emotional, and spiritual well-being. Are there any areas where you feel out of balance or in need of improvement?
As you embark on this journey, set specific, achievable goals for each aspect of your health and commit to working toward them over the next 40 days. Remember that you are not alone on this journey; God is with you every step of the way, providing guidance, strength, and support.

Lord Teach Me To	I Am Thankful For

Prayer

Heavenly Father, thank You for the gift of my body, mind, and soul. As I embark on this 40-day journey to holistic health, please guide me in making choices that honor You and support my overall well-being.

Help me to stay focused and committed to my goals, and grant me the wisdom and strength to overcome any challenges I may face along the way. In Jesus' name, I pray. **Amen.**

Day 2: Nourishing Your Body with Proper Nutrition

Reflection

Proper nutrition is a key component of a healthy, balanced lifestyle. It not only supports physical health but also affects your emotional and mental well-being. As you consider the role nutrition plays in your life, think about the choices you make daily in terms of the foods you consume.

Are they nourishing and beneficial to your body, or do they hinder your overall well-being?

This journey is an opportunity to learn more about the importance of nutrition and to make choices that honor your body as a temple of the Holy Spirit.

Bible Passage : Genesis 1:29 (NIV)

Then God said, "I give you every seed-bearing plant on the face of the whole earth and every tree that has fruit with seed in it. They will be yours for food."

Bible Passage : 1 Corinthians 10:31 (NIV)

So whether you eat or drink or whatever you do, do it all for the glory of God.

Application

Reflect on your current eating habits and how they align with a holistic approach to health. Are there areas where you can make improvements or incorporate more nourishing, whole foods?
Set achievable goals for incorporating healthier food choices into your daily routine, and seek out resources to help educate and guide you in making informed decisions about nutrition. Remember that this journey is not about deprivation, but about honoring your body and providing it with the nourishment it needs to thrive.

Lord Teach Me To

I Am Thankful For

Prayer

Lord, thank You for providing me with the nourishment I need to sustain my body and mind. As I embark on this journey to holistic health, guide me in making wise choices about the foods I consume. Help me to recognize that what I eat and drink is not only for my physical health but also a reflection of my relationship with You. Grant me the knowledge and discipline to make choices that honor my body as Your temple and support my overall well-being. In Jesus' name, I pray. **Amen.**

Day 3: The Importance of Physical Activity

Reflection

Physical activity is essential for maintaining a healthy body and mind. Regular exercise not only strengthens your muscles and improves cardio-vascular health, but it also helps reduce stress, improve sleep, and elevate mood.

As you reflect on the role of physical activity in your life, consider the various ways you can incorporate movement into your daily routine.

This journey is an opportunity to explore the many benefits of exercise and to discover activities that resonate with you and support your holistic health goals.

Bible Passage : 1 Timothy 4:8 (NIV)

For physical training is of some value, but godliness has value for all things, holding promise for both the present life and the life to come.

Bible Passage : 3 John 1:2 (NIV)

Dear friend, I pray that you may enjoy good health and that all may go well with you, even as your soul is getting along well.

Application

Reflect on your current level of physical activity and how it aligns with a holistic approach to health. Are there ways you can increase or diversify your exercise routine?

Set achievable goals for incorporating regular physical activity into your daily schedule, and explore different types of exercises to find what works best for you. Remember that the key to sustainable, long-term success is finding activities you enjoy and that support your overall well-being.

Lord Teach Me To

I Am Thankful For

Prayer

Lord, thank You for the gift of a healthy and capable body. As I work to strengthen and care for my physical self, please guide me in finding activities that promote health and well-being. Help me to recognize the importance of regular exercise and to make it a priority in my daily life. Grant me the discipline and motivation to maintain a consistent routine, and may I always be mindful of the connection between my physical health and spiritual well-being. In Jesus' name, I pray.**Amen.**

Day 4: Stress Management and Emotional Well-being

Reflection

Stress is an inevitable part of life, but how we respond to it can significantly impact our overall well-being.

Learning to manage stress effectively and cultivate emotional resilience is essential for holistic health. In today's reflection, consider the various sources of stress in your life and the strategies you can employ to cope with them.

Turning to prayer, meditation, and other spiritual practices can provide comfort, support, and guidance in challenging times.

Bible Passage : Philippians 4:6-7 (NIV)

Do not be anxious about anything, but in every situation, by prayer and petition, with thanksgiving, present your requests to God.

And the peace of God, which transcends all understanding, will guard your hearts and your minds in Christ Jesus.

Bible Passage : Proverbs 17:22 (NIV)

A cheerful heart is good medicine, but a crushed spirit dries up the bones.

Application

Reflect on your stress levels and the strategies you currently use to manage stress. Identify areas in your life where you can develop healthier coping mechanisms and establish a stress management routine.
This may include incorporating prayer, meditation, deep breathing, or other spiritual practices into your daily life. Additionally, consider seeking support from friends, family, or a professional counselor to help you navigate challenging situations and maintain emotional well-being.

Lord Teach Me To	I Am Thankful For

Prayer

Heavenly Father, I recognize that stress is a natural part of life, but I ask for Your guidance in managing it effectively. Help me to cultivate emotional resilience and to lean on You during times of difficulty.
Teach me to turn to prayer, meditation, and other spiritual practices as a means of finding comfort and support. Surround me with a loving community that can help me navigate the challenges of life and maintain a healthy balance between my emotional, physical, and spiritual well-being.
In Jesus' name, I pray.**Amen.**

Day 5: Achieving Mental Clarity and Focus

Reflection

Mental clarity and focus are essential for achieving our goals and living a fulfilled life.

However, distractions, stress, and an overactive mind can often hinder our ability to think clearly and maintain focus. In today's reflection, consider the factors that may be affecting your mental clarity and focus, and explore ways to enhance your cognitive function through mindfulness practices, proper nutrition, and other healthy habits.

Bible Passage : Romans 12:2 (NIV)

Do not conform to the pattern of this world, but be transformed by the renewing of your mind. Then you will be able to test and approve what

God's will is—his good, pleasing, and perfect will.

Bible Passage : Proverbs 4:25-27 (NIV)

Let your eyes look straight ahead; fix your gaze directly before you.

Give careful thought to the paths for your feet and be steadfast in all your ways.

Do not turn to the right or the left; keep your foot from evil.

Application

Reflect on your current mental clarity and focus. Identify factors that may be affecting your cognitive function, such as distractions, stress, or an unhealthy lifestyle. Consider incorporating mindfulness practices, such as meditation or prayer, into your daily routine to help you stay present and focused.

Additionally, examine your nutrition and sleep habits, as these can significantly impact your mental health. Make a plan to address any areas of concern and work toward improving your mental clarity and focus.

Lord Teach Me To	I Am Thankful For

Prayer

Lord, I ask for Your guidance in achieving mental clarity and focus. Help me identify and address the factors that may be affecting my cognitive function, and show me how to incorporate mindfulness practices, proper nutrition, and other healthy habits into my life.

Grant me the strength and discipline to make these changes for the betterment of my overall well-being. In Jesus' name, I pray.**Amen.**

Day 6: The Power of Prayer and Meditation

Reflection

Prayer and meditation are powerful tools for nurturing our spiritual well-being and enhancing our connection with God.

These practices help us develop inner peace, reduce stress, and cultivate a deep sense of gratitude and contentment.

As you reflect on your prayer and meditation practices, consider the ways in which they impact your daily life and overall well-being.

Bible Passage : Philippians 4:6-7 (NIV)

Do not be anxious about anything, but in every situation, by prayer and petition, with thanksgiving, present your requests to God.

And the peace of God, which transcends all understanding, will guard your hearts and your minds in Christ Jesus.

Bible Passage : Psalm 46:10 (NIV)

He says, "Be still, and know that I am God; I will be exalted among the nations, I will be exalted in the earth."

Application

Reflect on your current prayer and meditation practices. How do they help you connect with God and find inner peace? If you're not already incorporating these practices into your daily life, consider setting aside time each day for prayer and meditation. Start with just a few minutes, and gradually increase the duration as you become more comfortable. Remember, consistency is key to reaping the benefits of these spiritual practices.
As you deepen your connection with God, you'll likely experience increased peace, reduced stress, and a greater sense of overall well-being.

Lord Teach Me To

I Am Thankful For

Prayer

Heavenly Father, thank You for the gift of prayer and meditation. Please guide me as I seek to deepen my connection with You through these spiritual practices. Help me to find inner peace, reduce stress, and cultivate gratitude and contentment in my life.
Strengthen my commitment to nurturing my spiritual well-being, and may Your peace, which transcends all understanding, guard my heart and mind in Christ Jesus. **Amen.**

Day 7: Cultivating Gratitude and Positivity

Reflection

Gratitude and positivity play significant roles in our overall well-being.

By intentionally cultivating these qualities, we can transform our perspective on life, increase our happiness, and improve our mental and emotional health.

As you reflect on the ways you practice gratitude and positivity, consider how they affect your daily life and well-being.

Bible Passage : 1 Thessalonians 5:16-18 (NIV)

Rejoice always, pray continually, give thanks in all circumstances; for this is God's will for you in Christ Jesus.

Bible Passage : Philippians 4:8 (NIV)

Finally, brothers and sisters, whatever is true, whatever is noble, whatever is right, whatever is pure, whatever is lovely, whatever is admirable—if anything is excellent or praiseworthy—think about such things.

Application

Take a moment to reflect on your current attitude and mindset. How often do you practice gratitude and focus on positivity? Make a conscious effort to incorporate gratitude into your daily routine by creating a gratitude journal, expressing thanks in prayer, or simply taking a moment each day to acknowledge the good things in your life. Additionally, try to surround yourself with positivity by engaging with uplifting content, spending time with positive people, and reflecting on the positive aspects of your life. As you cultivate gratitude and positivity, you'll likely notice improvements in your overall well-being and a deeper sense of joy and fulfillment in your life.

Lord Teach Me To

I Am Thankful For

Prayer

Dear God, thank You for the countless blessings in my life. Help me to cultivate a heart of gratitude and a mindset of positivity. Teach me to focus on the good things in my life and to rejoice always, pray continually, and give thanks in all circumstances.
May my attitude and mindset be a reflection of Your love, grace, and goodness. In Jesus' name, **Amen.**

Day 8: Establishing Healthy Sleep Habits

Reflection

Sleep is a crucial component of holistic health.

Getting the right amount of rest each night allows our bodies to heal, our minds to process the day's events, and our spirits to rejuvenate. In today's fast-paced world, it can be challenging to prioritize sleep, but establishing healthy sleep habits can have a significant positive impact on our overall well-being.

Bible Passage : Psalm 127:2 (NIV)

In vain you rise early and stay up late, toiling for food to eat— for he grants sleep to those he loves.

Bible Passage : Proverbs 3:24 (NIV)

When you lie down, you will not be afraid; when you lie down, your sleep will be sweet.

Application

Evaluate your current sleep habits and determine if there are areas where you can make improvements. Consider establishing a bedtime routine that includes winding down activities, such as reading, prayer, or meditation, to signal your body and mind that it's time to rest. Prioritize a consistent sleep schedule, aiming for 7-9 hours of sleep per night. Finally, create a sleep-conducive environment by ensuring your bedroom is cool, dark, and quiet. As you make changes to your sleep habits, take note of how better quality sleep impacts your overall health and well-being.

Lord Teach Me To

I Am Thankful For

Prayer

Heavenly Father, thank You for the gift of rest and sleep. I ask for Your guidance as I work to establish healthy sleep habits.
Help me to prioritize rest and create an environment that promotes rejuvenating sleep. Grant me the wisdom to recognize the importance of sleep for my body, mind, and soul, and the discipline to make it a priority in my life. In Jesus' name, **Amen.**

Day 9: Building Strong Relationships and Community

Reflection

Building strong relationships and fostering a sense of community are essential aspects of holistic health.

Our connections with others provide us with emotional support, encouragement, and opportunities for personal growth.

By nurturing these relationships, we can experience a greater sense of belonging, happiness, and overall well-being.

Bible Passage : Hebrews 10:24-25 (NIV)

And let us consider how we may spur one another on toward love and good deeds, not giving up meeting together, as some are in the habit of doing, but encouraging one another—and all the more as you see the Day approaching.

Bible Passage : Proverbs 17:17 (NIV)

A friend loves at all times, and a brother is born for a time of adversity.

Application

Reflect on your current relationships and the sense of community in your life. Identify areas where you can invest more time and effort to strengthen these connections. Consider joining a local group or organization that aligns with your interests, such as a church group, volunteer organization, or social club.

Make an effort to be present and engaged when spending time with friends and family, and actively listen to their thoughts and feelings. Finally, practice kindness, empathy, and understanding in all your interactions to foster deeper connections and a strong sense of community.

Lord Teach Me To	I Am Thankful For

Prayer

Lord, thank You for the gift of relationships and community. Guide me as I strive to build stronger connections with those around me. Help me to be present, engaged, and empathetic in my interactions with others. Grant me the wisdom and courage to seek out new opportunities for personal growth and connection. In Your name, I pray. **Amen.**

Day 10: Honoring Your Body as a Temple

Reflection

Our bodies are incredibly complex and beautiful creations, and we must remember to treat them with the respect and care they deserve.

When we recognize our bodies as sacred temples, we can better understand the importance of nurturing and maintaining our physical health. Today, let us reflect on how we can honor our bodies and make choices that support our well-being.

Bible Passage : 1 Corinthians 6:19-20 (NIV)

Do you not know that your bodies are temples of the Holy Spirit, who is in you, whom you have received from God?

You are not your own; you were bought at a price.

Therefore honor God with your bodies.

Application

Take some time today to consider the ways in which you are currently honoring your body as a temple. Are there areas of your physical health that need improvement? Perhaps you need to make changes in your diet, exercise routine, or sleep habits. Consider creating a plan to address these areas and work toward a healthier lifestyle that honors your body as a sacred temple.

Additionally, take a moment to appreciate the incredible gift that is your body. Practice gratitude for all the things your body allows you to do and experience. Embrace self-compassion and love for your body, and remember that by caring for your physical health, you are also nurturing your spiritual well-being.

Lord Teach Me To

I Am Thankful For

Prayer

Heavenly Father, thank You for the gift of my body.

Help me to see it as a sacred temple and to treat it with the care and respect it deserves. Guide me in making choices that support my physical health and well-being, and let me always remember to honor You with my body. **Amen.**

Day 11: Discovering Your Spiritual Gifts

Reflection

God has blessed each of us with unique spiritual gifts that we can use to serve Him and others.

By discovering and embracing these gifts, we can experience a greater sense of purpose and fulfillment in our lives.

Today, let's reflect on our spiritual gifts and consider how we can use them to enrich our own lives and the lives of those around us.

Bible Passage : 1 Corinthians 12:4-11 (NIV)

There are different kinds of gifts, but the same Spirit distributes them.

There are different kinds of service, but the same Lord.

There are different kinds of working, but in all of them and in everyone it is the same God at work.

Now to each one the manifestation of the Spirit is given for the common good.

To one there is given through the Spirit a message of wisdom, to another a message of knowledge by means of the same Spirit, to another faith by the same Spirit, to another gifts of healing by that one Spirit, to another miraculous powers, to another prophecy, to another distinguishing between spirits, to another speaking in different kinds of tongues, and to still another the interpretation of tongues.

All these are the work of one and the same Spirit, and he distributes them to each one, just as he determines.

Application

Take some time today to reflect on your spiritual gifts. You may already have a clear understanding of your gifts, or you may need to spend time in prayer and self-examination to discern them. As you identify your gifts, consider how you can use them to serve God and others in your daily life.

If you're unsure of your spiritual gifts, consider taking a spiritual gifts assessment or talking with your pastor or a trusted friend for guidance. Once you have identified your gifts, create a plan to develop and utilize them in your personal, professional, and spiritual life. Remember that by embracing and using your spiritual gifts, you are not only enriching your own life but also contributing to the well-being of those around you.

Lord Teach Me To

I Am Thankful For

Prayer

Lord, thank You for the spiritual gifts You have bestowed upon me. Help me to recognize and develop these gifts so that I may use them to serve You and others.
Grant me the wisdom and guidance to utilize my gifts in a way that brings glory to Your name and enriches the lives of those around me. **Amen.**

Day 12: Practicing Forgiveness and Reconciliation

Reflection

Forgiveness and reconciliation play a vital role in our spiritual and emotional well-being. Holding onto resentment, anger, or bitterness can negatively impact our health and relationships.

Today, let's focus on the importance of practicing forgiveness and seeking reconciliation, both with ourselves and with others.

Bible Passage : Ephesians 4:31-32 (NIV)

Get rid of all bitterness, rage and anger, brawling and slander, along with every form of malice.

Be kind and compassionate to one another, forgiving each other, just as in Christ God forgave you.

Application

Take some time today to reflect on any situations or relationships in your life that may require forgiveness and reconciliation.

Consider the impact that holding onto negative emotions has had on your health and well-being.

Begin by forgiving yourself for any past mistakes or shortcomings, understanding that you are human and it's natural to make mistakes.

Next, identify any individuals with whom you need to seek forgiveness or offer forgiveness.

Remember, forgiveness doesn't mean forgetting or excusing the offense; it means releasing the burden of resentment and choosing to move forward.

Pray for the strength and courage to forgive and seek reconciliation.

Reach out to those you need to forgive or seek forgiveness from, and initiate a conversation to resolve any lingering issues.

By doing so, you'll experience a greater sense of peace and improved emotional well-being.

Lord Teach Me To	I Am Thankful For

Prayer

Heavenly Father, thank You for the gift of forgiveness that You have so graciously given us through Your Son, Jesus Christ.
Help me to practice forgiveness and reconciliation in my life, both with myself and with others.
Give me the strength and courage to let go of bitterness and resentment, and guide me in fostering healthy, loving relationships. **Amen.**

Day 13: Embracing the Healing Power of Nature

Reflection

Nature has a profound healing effect on our body, mind, and soul.

Spending time in nature can reduce stress, improve our mood, and promote a sense of well-being.

Today, let's explore the benefits of connecting with nature and ways to incorporate it into our daily lives.

Bible Passage : Psalm 19:1-4 (NIV)

The heavens declare the glory of God; the skies proclaim the work of his hands.

Day after day they pour forth speech; night after night they reveal knowledge.

They have no speech, they use no words; no sound is heard from them.

Yet their voice goes out into all the earth, their words to the ends of the world.

Application

Make an effort today to spend some time in nature, whether it's taking a walk in a park, sitting in your backyard, or going for a hike in the woods. As you do so, take note of the sights, sounds, and smells around you. Observe the beauty of creation and the calming effect it has on your mind and spirit.

Try to make spending time in nature a regular part of your routine. You can do this by scheduling regular walks, setting up an outdoor meditation spot, or simply taking a few minutes each day to appreciate the natural world around you. By doing so, you'll experience the healing power of nature and its positive impact on your holistic health.

Lord Teach Me To	I Am Thankful For

Prayer

Creator God, thank You for the beauty and healing power of nature that surrounds us. Help me to appreciate and connect with Your creation, and to embrace the benefits it offers to my body, mind, and soul.

Guide me in incorporating nature into my daily life, so I may experience the peace and well-being it provides. **Amen.**

Day 14: Overcoming Fears and Limiting Beliefs

Reflection

Fears and limiting beliefs can hold us back from reaching our full potential and enjoying a truly holistic, healthy life. It's essential to recognize and confront these fears, letting go of the beliefs that may be preventing us from living a fulfilling life.

Today, let's explore ways to overcome our fears and limiting beliefs and embrace the abundant life God has planned for us.

Bible Passage : 2 Timothy 1:7 (NIV)

For God has not given us a spirit of fear, but of power and of love and of a sound mind.

Application

Begin by identifying any fears or limiting beliefs that may be holding you back. These could be fears of failure, rejection, or even success.

Next, consider the root of these fears and how they may have developed. Reflect on past experiences or events that may have contributed to these beliefs.

Once you've identified your fears and limiting beliefs, turn to God in prayer, asking for the strength and wisdom to overcome them. Lean on His promises of love, power, and sound mind.

Replace your fears and limiting beliefs with faith, trust, and positive affirmations.

Find ways to confront your fears and challenge your limiting beliefs.

This could involve stepping out of your comfort zone, trying new experiences, or seeking support from friends, family, or a professional counselor.

By taking steps to overcome your fears and limiting beliefs, you'll open the door to a more fulfilling and holistic life.

Lord Teach Me To

I Am Thankful For

Prayer

Heavenly Father, I recognize the fears and limiting beliefs that hold me back from living the life You have planned for me. Help me to confront and overcome these fears, trusting in Your love, power, and sound mind.

Grant me the courage to challenge my limiting beliefs and to embrace the abundant life You have prepared for me. **Amen.**

Day 15: Developing a Personal Relationship with God

Reflection

Developing a personal relationship with God is at the core of a holistic, healthy life.

Through this relationship, we can find the guidance, support, and strength we need to overcome obstacles and live a life of purpose and fulfillment.

Today, let's explore ways to deepen our relationship with God and strengthen our spiritual health.

Bible Passage : Jeremiah 29:11-13 (NIV)

"For I know the plans I have for you," declares the Lord, "plans to prosper you and not to harm you, plans to give you hope and a future.

Then you will call on me and come and pray to me, and I will listen to you. You will seek me and find me when you seek me with all your heart."

Application

To develop a personal relationship with God, it's essential to cultivate a consistent prayer life.

Set aside time each day to communicate with God, sharing your thoughts, feelings, and concerns, and listening for His guidance.

Make Bible study a regular part of your daily routine. The more you read and understand God's Word, the more you'll gain insight into His character and His will for your life.
Consider joining a Bible study group or seeking out resources to help deepen your understanding of Scripture.

Worship and fellowship with other believers are also crucial components of a strong relationship with God.

Attend church services and participate in community events to grow in your faith and connect with others who share your beliefs.

Lastly, practice living out your faith by being a reflection of God's love in your daily actions and interactions with others.

Serve others, show kindness, and strive to be a positive influence in the lives of those around you.

Lord Teach Me To

I Am Thankful For

Prayer

Dear Lord, I desire to deepen my relationship with You and strengthen my spiritual health. Guide me as I seek to develop a consistent prayer life, study Your Word, and connect with other believers.

Help me to live out my faith each day, reflecting Your love and grace to those around me **Amen.**

Day 16: The Role of Mindfulness in Holistic Health

Reflection

Mindfulness is the practice of being fully present and aware of our thoughts, feelings, and bodily sensations without judgment. Incorporating mindfulness into our daily lives can have a profound impact on our overall well-being, helping us to better manage stress, improve mental clarity, and cultivate a deeper connection with ourselves and the world around us.

Today, we'll explore the role of mindfulness in holistic health and how it can support our spiritual journey.

Bible Passage : Psalm 46:10 (NIV)

"Be still, and know that I am God; I will be exalted among the nations, I will be exalted in the earth."

Application

Practicing mindfulness can take many forms, and you can choose the techniques that resonate best with you. Some ways to incorporate mindfulness into your daily routine include:

Mindful breathing: Focus on your breath as you inhale and exhale, bringing your attention back to your breath whenever your mind wanders. This practice can help you find calm and presence in the midst of daily stresses.

Mindful eating: Pay close attention to the flavors, textures, and sensations of your food as you eat. This practice can help you cultivate gratitude and deepen your connection with the nourishment your body receives.

Mindful walking: Practice being fully present as you walk, taking note of your surroundings and the sensation of each step. This can be a grounding and meditative experience.

Mindful meditation: Set aside time each day for a focused meditation practice, during which you gently observe your thoughts, feelings, and sensations without judgment.

As you incorporate mindfulness practices into your life, you'll likely find that your connection to God deepens as well.
By learning to be still and present, you create space for God to speak to your heart and guide your steps.

Lord Teach Me To

I Am Thankful For

Prayer

Heavenly Father, thank You for the gift of mindfulness and its role in holistic health.
Teach me to be present and aware in each moment, creating space for Your guidance and wisdom. Help me to embrace mindfulness practices that support my spiritual journey and deepen my connection with You.
Amen.

Day 17: The Art of Loving Yourself and Others

Reflection

To love ourselves and others is a cornerstone of holistic health.

Embracing self-love allows us to cultivate a positive relationship with ourselves, which in turn enables us to love others more fully.

Recognizing that we are all created in the image of God and deserving of love is a vital step in fostering spiritual growth and well-being.

Bible Passage : Mark 12:30-31 (NIV)

"Love the Lord your God with all your heart and with all your soul and with all your mind and with all your strength."

"The second is this: 'Love your neighbor as yourself.' There is no commandment greater than these."

Application

Here are some ways to practice the art of loving yourself and others:

Be kind to yourself: Treat yourself with the same compassion and understanding you would offer to a close friend. Speak positively to yourself and celebrate your accomplishments, no matter how small.

Prioritize self-care: Invest time and energy in activities that nourish your body, mind, and soul. By taking care of yourself, you'll be better equipped to care for others.

Forgive yourself and others: Let go of past mistakes and grudges, recognizing that we are all imperfect beings on a journey of growth and learning.

Practice empathy: Put yourself in someone else's shoes and strive to understand their feelings, thoughts, and experiences.

Offer support and encouragement: Be a source of light and love for those around you, lifting others up and offering a helping hand when needed.

As you cultivate love for yourself and others, you'll find that your spiritual and emotional well-being flourishes.
Remember, we are called to love our neighbors as ourselves, and doing so brings us closer to God's divine plan for our lives.

Lord Teach Me To	I Am Thankful For

Prayer

Lord, thank You for the gift of love and the opportunity to share it with others. Teach me to love myself and others in a way that reflects Your love for us.

Help me to embrace self-compassion, forgiveness, empathy, and encouragement as I walk this journey of holistic health. **Amen.**

Day 18: Setting Boundaries and Prioritizing Self-Care

Reflection

Establishing healthy boundaries and prioritizing self-care are essential aspects of holistic health.
Boundaries allow us to maintain balance in our lives, protect our well-being, and honor our personal values.
Prioritizing self-care means investing in activities and habits that nurture our bodies, minds, and souls.

By creating and maintaining boundaries and making self-care a priority, we can achieve a greater sense of harmony and well-being.

Bible Passage : Matthew 11:28-30 (NIV)

"Come to me, all you who are weary and burdened, and I will give you rest. Take my yoke upon you and learn from me, for I am gentle and humble in heart, and you will find rest for your souls.

For my yoke is easy and my burden is light."

Application

To set boundaries and prioritize self-care, consider the following steps:

Identify your values: Determine what is most important to you, and use these values as a guide for making decisions about your time, energy, and resources.

Learn to say no: Recognize that it's okay to decline requests that conflict with your values, drain your energy, or negatively affect your well-being.

Schedule self-care: Set aside regular time for activities that nourish your body, mind, and soul. This may include exercise, prayer, meditation, hobbies, or spending time with loved ones.

Communicate your needs: Be open and honest with others about your boundaries and self-care needs, explaining the importance of these practices for your overall well-being.

Seek support: Surround yourself with people who respect your boundaries and encourage your self-care efforts.

As you set boundaries and prioritize self-care, remember that God wants you to care for yourself, so you can be a vessel of His love and light to others.

Lord Teach Me To	I Am Thankful For

Prayer

Heavenly Father, help me to establish healthy boundaries and prioritize self-care in my life.
Grant me the wisdom to recognize my values and the courage to uphold them.
Teach me to seek rest in You, and guide me in nurturing my body, mind, and soul. **Amen.**

Day 19: The Importance of Spiritual Disciplines

Reflection

Spiritual disciplines are practices that help us connect with God, nurture our spiritual growth, and deepen our relationship with Him.
They are essential for maintaining our spiritual health and achieving holistic well-being. Some common spiritual disciplines include prayer, meditation, Bible study, fasting, worship, and service.

By engaging in these practices consistently, we can draw closer to God, cultivate spiritual maturity, and experience greater peace and joy in our lives.

Bible Passage : 1 Timothy 4:7-8 (NIV)

Have nothing to do with godless myths and old wives' tales; rather, train yourself to be godly.

For physical training is of some value, but godliness has value for all things, holding promise for both the present life and the life to come.

Application

To incorporate spiritual disciplines into your life, consider the following steps:

Start with prayer: Begin each day by asking God for guidance and strength as you engage in spiritual disciplines.

Choose a few disciplines to focus on: Select a few practices that resonate with you and commit to incorporating them into your daily or weekly routine.

Create a spiritual growth plan: Set specific goals for each discipline and establish a schedule to help you stay on track.

Be consistent: Consistency is key to experiencing the benefits of spiritual disciplines.
Even if you miss a day or encounter obstacles, keep persevering.

Reflect on your progress: Regularly assess your growth in each discipline, celebrate your successes, and make adjustments as needed.

As you engage in spiritual disciplines, remember that the ultimate goal is not merely to check off a list of tasks, but to deepen your relationship with God and experience His transforming power in your life.

Lord Teach Me To	I Am Thankful For

Prayer

Lord, thank You for the gift of spiritual disciplines that help me grow closer to You. Guide me as I seek to incorporate these practices into my life and develop a deeper relationship with You.

Help me to be consistent and intentional in my pursuit of godliness, and transform me into the person You desire me to be. **Amen.**

Day 20: Cultivating Joy and Contentment

Reflection

Joy and contentment are essential components of holistic health.
They provide a sense of inner peace and well-being, regardless of our external circumstances.
Cultivating joy and contentment involves recognizing and appreciating the blessings in our lives, choosing to focus on the positive, and trusting God in all situations.
By developing an attitude of gratitude and maintaining a strong connection with our Creator, we can experience genuine happiness that transcends our circumstances.

Bible Passage : Philippians 4:11-13 (NIV)

I am not saying this because I am in need, for I have learned to be content whatever the circumstances.
I know what it is to be in need, and I know what it is to have plenty. I have learned the secret of being content in any and every situation, whether well fed or hungry, whether living in plenty or in want.
I can do all this through him who gives me strength.

Application

To cultivate joy and contentment in your life, consider the following steps:

Practice gratitude: Each day, take a moment to reflect on the blessings in your life and express your gratitude to God for His provision and care.

Focus on the positive: Rather than dwelling on negative thoughts or circumstances, choose to focus on the positive aspects of your life and the goodness of God.

Surrender to God: Trust that God is in control of your life and that He is working for your good, even when circumstances are challenging.

Cultivate a joyful mindset: Make a conscious effort to find joy in every situation, even when things are not going as planned.

Surround yourself with positivity: Spend time with people who uplift and encourage you, and engage in activities that bring you happiness and fulfillment.

As you intentionally focus on cultivating joy and contentment, you will experience a deeper sense of well-being and a more abundant life.

Lord Teach Me To	I Am Thankful For

Prayer

Heavenly Father, thank You for the gift of joy and contentment that comes from knowing You. Help me to cultivate a grateful heart and a positive mindset, trusting in Your goodness and provision in every circumstance.
Teach me to find joy in the journey and to rely on Your strength to overcome challenges and obstacles. May my life be a testimony to Your grace and an inspiration to others. **Amen.**

Day 21: Embracing Vulnerability and Authenticity

Reflection

Vulnerability and authenticity are key aspects of holistic health, as they allow us to connect more deeply with ourselves, others, and God.

Embracing vulnerability means being willing to open up about our fears, struggles, and imperfections, while authenticity involves living true to our values and beliefs.

By allowing ourselves to be vulnerable and authentic, we can foster genuine connections and experience personal growth.

Bible Passage : 2 Corinthians 12:9-10 (NIV)

But he said to me, "My grace is sufficient for you, for my power is made perfect in weakness." Therefore I will boast all the more gladly about my weaknesses, so that Christ's power may rest on me.
That is why, for Christ's sake, I delight in weaknesses, in insults, in hardships, in persecutions, in difficulties. For when I am weak, then I am strong.

Application

To embrace vulnerability and authenticity in your life, consider the following steps:

Acknowledge your emotions: Allow yourself to feel and express your emotions, both positive and negative, without judgment or suppression.

Share your struggles: Open up to trusted friends or family members about your challenges and fears, and seek their support and encouragement.

Accept your imperfections: Recognize that you are not perfect and that it's okay to make mistakes, learn from them, and grow.

Live in alignment with your values: Make decisions and take actions that reflect your core beliefs and values, even when it's difficult or unpopular.

Practice self-compassion: Treat yourself with kindness, understanding, and forgiveness, recognizing that you are a work in progress.

As you embrace vulnerability and authenticity, you will deepen your relationships, enhance your spiritual growth, and experience greater personal fulfillment.

Lord Teach Me To	I Am Thankful For

Prayer

Lord, thank You for loving me despite my weaknesses and imperfections. Help me to embrace vulnerability and authenticity in my life, allowing Your grace and power to shine through my struggles.
Teach me to live in alignment with my values and beliefs and to practice self-compassion as I continue on my journey toward holistic health.
May my openness and authenticity inspire and encourage others in their own journeys. **Amen.**

Day 22: The Power of Positive Affirmations

Reflection

Vulnerability and authenticity are key aspects of holistic health, as they allow us to connect more deeply with ourselves, others, and God.

Embracing vulnerability means being willing to open up about our fears, struggles, and imperfections, while authenticity involves living true to our values and beliefs.

By allowing ourselves to be vulnerable and authentic, we can foster genuine connections and experience personal growth.

Bible Passage : Proverbs 18:21 (NIV)

The tongue has the power of life and death, and those who love it will eat its fruit.

Application

To harness the power of positive affirmations, follow these steps:

Identify negative thought patterns: Recognize the negative thoughts and beliefs that may be holding you back from experiencing joy and fulfillment.

Create positive affirmations: Replace these negative thoughts with positive, empowering statements that affirm your worth, capabilities, and potential. Ensure that your affirmations are present tense, specific, and realistic.

Practice regularly: Repeat your affirmations daily, either silently or aloud, ideally in front of a mirror. You can also write them down in a journal or post them in visible places as reminders.

Believe in your affirmations: Embrace the truth of your affirmations, trusting that they reflect your true nature and abilities.

Be patient: Understand that change takes time, and it may take several weeks or months for your thought patterns to shift.

Examples of positive affirmations include:

I am loved, valued, and worthy.
I am strong and resilient.
I am capable of achieving my goals and dreams.
I am grateful for the blessings in my life.
I am growing and learning every day.

As you practice positive affirmations, you'll notice improvements in your self-esteem, outlook on life, and overall well-being.

Lord Teach Me To	I Am Thankful For

Prayer

Heavenly Father, thank You for the power of our words and thoughts. Help me to recognize and replace any negative thought patterns with positive affirmations that reflect Your love and truth.

May these affirmations guide me toward a more optimistic outlook and a deeper sense of self-worth. I trust in Your grace and guidance as I continue on my journey toward holistic health. **Amen.**

Day 23: Finding Purpose and Passion in Life

Reflection

Discovering your purpose and passion in life is essential for achieving holistic health.
When you are clear about your purpose, you can live a more intentional, fulfilling life that aligns with your values and beliefs.
Your passion can energize and motivate you, as well as bring joy and satisfaction to your daily experiences.
By pursuing your purpose and passion, you can nurture your spiritual, mental, and emotional well-being and create a more meaningful life.

Bible Passage : Ephesians 2:10 (NIV)

For we are God's handiwork, created in Christ Jesus to do good works, which God prepared in advance for us to do.

Application

To help you discover your purpose and passion, consider the following steps:

Reflect on your values: Identify your core values and beliefs, and consider how they align with your current life choices and decisions.

Identify your strengths and talents: Assess your natural abilities, skills, and gifts that you can use to make a positive impact in the world.

Explore your interests: Consider activities, hobbies, and subjects that bring you joy, excitement, and satisfaction.

Seek God's guidance: Pray for clarity, wisdom, and guidance as you seek to understand your purpose and passion.

Set goals and take action: Once you have identified your purpose and passion, set realistic and achievable goals that align with your values and strengths. Take action toward these goals, trusting that God will guide and support you.

As you pursue your purpose and passion, you will experience a deeper sense of fulfillment, joy, and spiritual growth in your life.

Lord Teach Me To	I Am Thankful For

Prayer

Dear God, thank You for creating me with unique strengths, talents, and passions. Please guide me as I seek to discover my purpose in life and use my gifts to serve You and others.
Help me to align my life with my values and beliefs, and to live each day with intention and meaning. I trust in Your guidance and provision as I pursue my passion and purpose, and I ask for Your strength and wisdom as I journey toward holistic health. **Amen.**

Day 24: Surrendering Your Worries and Anxieties to God

Reflection

Worries and anxieties can take a toll on your mental, emotional, and spiritual well-being. Learning to surrender your worries and anxieties to God is essential for maintaining holistic health.

By trusting in God's love, care, and wisdom, you can experience greater peace, security, and serenity in your daily life.

Bible Passage : 1 Peter 5:6-7 (NIV)

Humble yourselves, therefore, under God's mighty hand, that he may lift you up in due time.

Cast all your anxiety on him because he cares for you.

Application

To help you surrender your worries and anxieties to God, consider the following steps:

Acknowledge your feelings: Recognize and admit your anxieties and worries. Be honest with yourself and with God about the concerns that weigh on your heart.

Reflect on God's promises: Remind yourself of God's faithfulness, love, and care. Read and meditate on scriptures that speak to God's provision, protection, and guidance.

Pray for peace and trust: Bring your worries and anxieties to God in prayer. Ask for peace, strength, and trust in His divine plan for your life.

Release your concerns: Visualize yourself handing over your anxieties and worries to God. Trust that He is in control and will provide for you in every situation.

Cultivate gratitude: Focus on the blessings in your life and express gratitude to God for His goodness, love, and care.

By surrendering your worries and anxieties to God, you can experience a deeper sense of peace and well-being in your life.

Lord Teach Me To	I Am Thankful For

Prayer

Heavenly Father, I come before You with my worries and anxieties. I acknowledge that they weigh heavily on my heart, and I ask for Your help in surrendering them to You. Thank You for Your unfailing love and care, and for Your promises to provide, protect, and guide me.
Grant me peace and trust in Your divine plan for my life. Help me to cultivate gratitude for Your blessings and to experience a deeper sense of peace and well-being as I trust in You. **Amen.**

Day 25: Overcoming Negative Thought Patterns

Reflection

Negative thought patterns can significantly impact your emotional, mental, and spiritual well-being. To achieve holistic health, it's essential to address and overcome these negative thoughts.

By becoming aware of your thought patterns and replacing them with positive, uplifting thoughts, you can promote better emotional and mental health.

Bible Passage : Philippians 4:8 (NIV)

Finally, brothers and sisters, whatever is true, whatever is noble, whatever is right, whatever is pure, whatever is lovely, whatever is admirable—if anything is excellent or praiseworthy—think about such things.

Application

To overcome negative thought patterns, consider the following steps:

Identify your negative thoughts: Be aware of the thoughts that trigger negative emotions or reactions. Recognize the situations in which these thoughts occur.
Challenge your negative thoughts: Question the validity of your negative thoughts. Are they based on facts or assumptions? Are they exaggerated or distorted?
Replace negative thoughts with positive ones: Replace each negative thought with a positive, uplifting, or encouraging thought. Look for evidence that supports the positive thought and challenges the negative one.
Practice mindfulness: Develop a regular mindfulness practice to help you become more aware of your thoughts and emotions. This can help you recognize negative thought patterns and choose to focus on positive thoughts instead.

- **Seek support:** Talk to a trusted friend, family member, or counselor about your negative thought patterns. They can provide insight, encouragement, and support as you work to overcome them.

By addressing and overcoming negative thought patterns, you can improve your emotional and mental well-being, contributing to your overall holistic health.

Lord Teach Me To	I Am Thankful For

Prayer

Heavenly Father, I ask for Your guidance as I work to overcome negative thought patterns in my life. Help me to identify these thoughts and replace them with positive, uplifting ones.
Give me the strength and wisdom to challenge my negative thoughts and focus on what is true, noble, right, pure, lovely, and admirable. Thank You for Your constant presence and support in my journey toward holistic health. **Amen.**

Day 26: Nurturing Your Creativity and Imagination

Reflection

Creativity and imagination are essential aspects of our well-being, allowing us to express ourselves and explore our inner world.

Nurturing these qualities helps promote emotional, mental, and spiritual growth, contributing to our holistic health. Embrace your creative side, and find ways to express and celebrate your unique gifts and talents.

Bible Passage : Exodus 35:31-33 (NIV)

And he has filled him with the Spirit of God, with wisdom, with understanding, with knowledge and with all kinds of skills— to make artistic designs for work in gold, silver and bronze, to cut and set stones, to work in wood and to engage in all kinds of artistic crafts.

Application

To nurture your creativity and imagination, consider the following suggestions:
Engage in creative activities: Find a creative outlet that brings you joy and allows you to express yourself. This could include painting, drawing, writing, dancing, playing an instrument, or any other creative pursuit.

Make time for play: Allow yourself the freedom to explore and experiment without judgment. Play encourages creativity and can help you reconnect with your imaginative side.

Seek inspiration: Surround yourself with things that inspire you, such as art, music, books, or nature. Look for inspiration in everyday life, and be open to new ideas and perspectives.

Challenge yourself: Push yourself to try new things, and don't be afraid to take risks. Stepping out of your comfort zone can help you grow creatively and expand your imagination.

Connect with others: Share your creative work with others and seek out like-minded individuals who can encourage and support your creative journey.

By nurturing your creativity and imagination, you can enhance your emotional, mental, and spiritual well-being, contributing to your overall holistic health.

Lord Teach Me To	I Am Thankful For

Prayer

Lord, thank You for the gift of creativity and imagination. Help me to embrace my unique talents and find ways to express and celebrate them.

Guide me as I seek inspiration and challenge myself to grow creatively. May my creative journey bring me closer to You and contribute to my holistic health. **Amen.**

Day 27: Cultivating Resilience and Perseverance

Reflection

Resilience and perseverance are vital qualities for our holistic health, as they help us navigate life's challenges and remain steadfast in our personal growth.

By cultivating these traits, we can better adapt to change, overcome obstacles, and continue moving forward on our spiritual journey.

Bible Passage : James 1:2-4 (NIV)

Consider it pure joy, my brothers and sisters, whenever you face trials of many kinds, because you know that the testing of your faith produces perseverance.
Let perseverance finish its work so that you may be mature and complete, not lacking anything.

Application

To cultivate resilience and perseverance, consider the following suggestions:
Embrace challenges: View obstacles and setbacks as opportunities for growth and learning. Try to approach them with a positive attitude and a willingness to adapt and overcome.
Develop a support network: Surround yourself with friends, family, and mentors who can offer encouragement, guidance, and support during difficult times.

Practice self-compassion: Be kind to yourself when you face setbacks or failures. Remember that everyone experiences challenges, and it's important to treat yourself with the same understanding and compassion you would offer to others.

Reflect on past successes: Remind yourself of times when you've overcome challenges and demonstrated resilience. Use these experiences to bolster your confidence and inspire you to keep moving forward.

Strengthen your faith: Turn to prayer, meditation, and Scripture for guidance and strength during difficult times. Trust in God's plan for your life, and lean on your faith to help you persevere through challenges.

By cultivating resilience and perseverance, you can better navigate life's challenges and continue on your spiritual journey toward holistic health.

Lord Teach Me To	I Am Thankful For

Prayer

Heavenly Father, thank You for the challenges that help me grow and become more resilient. Help me to embrace these trials with a positive attitude and trust in Your plan for my life.

Strengthen my faith, and guide me as I cultivate resilience and perseverance. May these qualities contribute to my holistic health and bring me closer to You. **Amen.**

Day 28: Practicing Patience and Trust in God's Timing

Reflection

Patience and trust in God's timing are essential elements for our holistic health. In a world that often values speed and instant gratification, learning to be patient and trusting in God's plan for our lives can bring us peace, reduce stress, and deepen our relationship with our Creator.

Bible Passage : Psalm 27:13-14 (NIV)

I remain confident of this: I will see the goodness of the Lord in the land of the living.

Wait for the Lord; be strong and take heart and wait for the Lord.

Application

To practice patience and trust in God's timing, consider the following suggestions:

Meditate on Scripture: Reflect on Bible passages that discuss patience and God's timing, such as Psalm 27:14, Ecclesiastes 3:1, and Isaiah 40:31.

Pray for patience: Ask God to grant you the patience and trust needed to navigate life's challenges and to accept His timing.

Cultivate mindfulness: Practice mindfulness techniques, such as deep breathing and meditation, to help you stay present and focused on the current moment.

Set realistic expectations: Recognize that life is full of unexpected twists and turns, and adjust your expectations accordingly. Understand that God's plan for your life may not always align with your own timeline.

Be patient with yourself and others: Practice patience in your daily interactions with yourself and those around you. Remember that everyone is on their own journey, and we all experience growth and change at different rates.

By practicing patience and trusting in God's timing, you can experience greater peace and contentment in your life and continue on your spiritual journey toward holistic health.

Lord Teach Me To	I Am Thankful For

Prayer

Lord, thank You for the reminder that Your timing is perfect, and Your plans for my life are greater than my own. Help me to be patient and to trust in Your timing, even when life doesn't unfold as I expect.

Grant me the wisdom and strength to accept Your will and to walk confidently in the path You've laid out for me. **Amen.**

Day 29: Embracing Change and Personal Growth

Reflection

Change is an inevitable part of life, and personal growth often occurs as we navigate these changes.

Embracing change and using it as an opportunity for growth can help us become more adaptable and resilient individuals.

By trusting in God's guidance and seeking His wisdom, we can find the strength to face life's challenges and evolve into the best versions of ourselves.

Bible Passage : Philippians 4:12-13 (NIV)

I know what it is to be in need, and I know what it is to have plenty.
I have learned the secret of being content in any and every situation, whether well fed or hungry, whether living in plenty or in want.

I can do all this through Him who gives me strength.

Application

To embrace change and personal growth, consider the following suggestions:

Reflect on past experiences: Look back on the changes you've experienced in your life and consider how they have shaped you and contributed to your growth.

Seek God's guidance: Pray for wisdom and guidance in navigating change and growth. Trust that God has a plan for your life and will provide the strength you need to face challenges.

Be open to new experiences: Approach change with an open mind and a willingness to learn from new experiences.

Develop healthy coping strategies: Learn and practice healthy ways to cope with stress, anxiety, and uncertainty.

Surround yourself with supportive people: Cultivate relationships with people who support and encourage your personal growth.

By embracing change and seeking personal growth, you can continue on your journey toward holistic health and deepen your relationship with God.

Lord Teach Me To	I Am Thankful For

Prayer

Heavenly Father, thank You for the opportunities for growth that change brings. Help me to trust in Your guidance as I navigate the changes in my life and to embrace them as opportunities for growth.
Give me the strength and courage to face challenges and the wisdom to learn from my experiences. Surround me with supportive people who will encourage me on my journey toward holistic health.
In Jesus' name, I pray. **Amen.**

Day 30: The Power of Silence and Solitude

Reflection

In our fast-paced world, silence and solitude can be rare and valuable gifts.

By intentionally setting aside time for quiet reflection and introspection, we can deepen our relationship with God, gain clarity on our life's purpose, and cultivate inner peace.

Embracing silence and solitude can help us develop a more mindful and balanced approach to life, enhancing our overall well-being.

Bible Passage : Psalm 46:10 (NIV)

He says, "Be still, and know that I am God; I will be exalted among the nations, I will be exalted in the earth."

Application

To experience the power of silence and solitude, try the following:

Set aside regular time for silence and solitude: Carve out time in your daily or weekly schedule for quiet reflection and introspection.

Create a sacred space: Designate a specific place in your home or elsewhere where you can go to be alone with your thoughts and with God.

Limit distractions: Turn off electronic devices, and minimize noise and other distractions during your time of silence and solitude.

Practice mindfulness: Focus on your breath and bodily sensations as you sit in silence. This will help to calm your mind and create a deeper connection with your inner self and God.

Engage in prayer and meditation: Use this time to pray, meditate on Scripture, or simply be present with God.

As you incorporate silence and solitude into your life, you will likely find a greater sense of inner peace, clarity, and spiritual growth.

Lord Teach Me To	I Am Thankful For

Prayer

Lord, thank You for the gift of silence and solitude. Help me to set aside regular time for quiet reflection and to create a sacred space where I can be alone with You.

Teach me to be still and know that You are God, and guide me as I seek to cultivate inner peace and spiritual growth. In Jesus' name, I pray.**Amen.**

Day 31: Achieving Balance in All Aspects of Life

Reflection

Achieving balance in all aspects of life is essential for holistic health. When we find harmony between our physical, mental, emotional, and spiritual selves, we can experience a deeper sense of well-being and fulfillment.

Striving for balance helps us to avoid burnout, maintain healthy relationships, and prioritize self-care. It also enables us to lead a more productive and meaningful life.

Bible Passage : Ecclesiastes 3:1-8 (NIV)

There is a time for everything, and a season for every activity under the heavens: a time to be born and a time to die, a time to plant and a time to uproot, a time to kill and a time to heal, a time to tear down and a time to build, a time to weep and a time to laugh, a time to mourn and a time to dance, a time to scatter stones and a time to gather them, a time to embrace and a time to refrain from embracing, a time to search and a time to give up, a time to keep and a time to throw away, a time to tear and a time to mend, a time to be silent and a time to speak, a time to love and a time to hate, a time for war and a time for peace.

Application

To achieve balance in all aspects of life, consider the following:

Set realistic goals: Set achievable goals for different areas of your life, such as health, relationships, career, and spirituality. Break your goals into smaller, manageable steps to avoid overwhelm and increase the likelihood of success.

Prioritize self-care: Make time for activities that nourish your body, mind, and soul. This could include exercise, healthy eating, prayer, meditation, and spending time in nature.

Establish boundaries: Learn to say "no" to activities and commitments that do not align with your priorities and values. Set limits on work and personal obligations to create a healthy balance.

Cultivate strong relationships: Invest time and energy in nurturing relationships with family, friends, and community members. Strong connections can provide support and encouragement as you work toward achieving balance in your life.

Practice gratitude: Focus on the blessings in your life and express gratitude for them. This can help you maintain a positive outlook and foster a sense of balance and contentment.

Seek guidance from God: Pray for wisdom and direction as you strive to achieve balance in your life. Trust in God's plan for you and rely on His strength to help you find harmony in all aspects of your life.

Lord Teach Me To	I Am Thankful For

Prayer

Heavenly Father, thank You for Your guidance as I seek to achieve balance in all aspects of my life. Help me to set realistic goals, prioritize self-care, establish boundaries, cultivate strong relationships, and practice gratitude.
I trust in Your plan for my life and ask for Your strength and wisdom as I strive for harmony in my physical, mental, emotional, and spiritual well-being. In Jesus' name, I pray. **Amen.**

Day 32: The Importance of Compassion and Empathy

Reflection

Compassion and empathy are essential for cultivating healthy relationships, deepening our spiritual lives, and fostering personal growth.

They enable us to better understand the feelings and experiences of others, offer support and encouragement, and demonstrate God's love to those around us.

By practicing compassion and empathy, we not only improve our own emotional well-being but also contribute to the well-being of others.

Bible Passage : Colossians 3:12-14 (NIV)

Therefore, as God's chosen people, holy and dearly loved, clothe yourselves with compassion, kindness, humility, gentleness, and patience.
Bear with each other and forgive one another if any of you has a grievance against someone. Forgive as the Lord forgave you.
And over all these virtues put on love, which binds them all together in perfect unity.

Application

To cultivate compassion and empathy in your life, consider the following:

Listen actively: When someone shares their feelings or experiences with you, listen attentively without interrupting or judging. Practice active listening by reflecting back on what the person has said, asking open-ended questions, and offering words of support and understanding.
Put yourself in their shoes: Try to imagine what it might feel like to be in the other person's situation. This can help you develop empathy and understanding for their experiences and emotions.
Offer support: When someone is facing a difficult situation, offer your assistance or encouragement. This could include practical help, emotional support, or simply being present and available to listen.
Practice forgiveness: Remember that everyone makes mistakes and faces challenges in their lives. Be willing to forgive others for their shortcomings and strive to treat them with kindness and understanding.

Cultivate self-compassion: Recognize that you, too, deserve compassion and understanding. Treat yourself with kindness, especially during times of struggle or self-doubt.

Pray for others: Regularly pray for the well-being and needs of others, asking God to provide comfort, strength, and guidance in their lives.

Lord Teach Me To	I Am Thankful For

Prayer

Lord, thank You for the gift of compassion and empathy. Help me to listen actively, put myself in the shoes of others, offer support, and practice forgiveness.

Teach me to cultivate self-compassion and to pray for the needs of those around me. May I become a reflection of Your love and compassion to others, and may my actions contribute to the well-being of both myself and those I encounter. In Jesus' name, I pray. **Amen.**

Day 33: Living a Life of Generosity and Service

Reflection

Living a life of generosity and service not only benefits others but also enriches our own lives.

By giving of our time, talents, and resources, we demonstrate love, compassion, and gratitude.

Furthermore, serving others can deepen our connection with God and foster a sense of purpose and fulfillment in our lives.

Bible Passage : Acts 20:35 (NIV)

In everything I did, I showed you that by this kind of hard work we must help the weak, remembering the words the Lord Jesus himself said: 'It is more blessed to give than to receive.'

Application

To embrace generosity and service in your life, consider the following:
Reflect on your blessings: Acknowledge the gifts, talents, and resources you possess and be grateful for them. This awareness can inspire you to share your blessings with others.

Identify your passions: Consider the causes, issues, or needs that resonate with your heart. By focusing on areas you are passionate about, you can make a more significant impact and find greater joy in serving others.

Volunteer your time and talents: Seek opportunities to volunteer in your community, at your place of worship, or with a local nonprofit organization. This can provide valuable experiences and connections while making a positive impact on the lives of others.

Practice financial generosity: Make regular contributions to charities, causes, or individuals in need. This not only benefits others but also fosters a spirit of gratitude and abundance in your own life.

Offer emotional support: Be available to listen, encourage, and support others in times of need. This can provide a valuable lifeline for someone facing difficult circumstances.

Pray for opportunities to serve: Ask God to open your eyes to the needs around you and to guide you in how you can best support and serve others.

Lord Teach Me To	I Am Thankful For

Prayer

Heavenly Father, thank You for the blessings You have bestowed upon me. Help me to recognize the gifts, talents, and resources I possess and to use them for the benefit of others. Guide me as I seek to live a life of generosity and service, and may my actions bring glory to Your name. Open my eyes to the needs around me and grant me the wisdom and courage to serve others with love and compassion.
In Jesus' name, I pray. **Amen.**

Day 34: The Role of Intuition in Holistic Health

Reflection

Intuition is often described as the ability to understand or know something without conscious reasoning. It's a gut feeling, an inner voice, or a sense of guidance that comes from within. In the context of holistic health, intuition can play a crucial role in helping us make decisions that promote our well-being and spiritual growth.
By learning to trust and develop our intuition, we can gain insight into our physical, emotional, and spiritual needs and become more attuned to the guidance of God and our inner selves.

Bible Passage : 1 Kings 19:11-13 (NIV)

The Lord said, "Go out and stand on the mountain in the presence of the Lord, for the Lord is about to pass by." Then a great and powerful wind tore the mountains apart and shattered the rocks before the Lord, but the Lord was not in the wind. After the wind, there was an earthquake, but the Lord was not in the earthquake. After the earthquake came a fire, but the Lord was not in the fire. And after the fire came a gentle whisper. When Elijah heard it, he pulled his cloak over his face and went out and stood at the mouth of the cave.
Then a voice said to him, "What are you doing here, Elijah?"

Application

To develop and trust your intuition in the context of holistic health, consider these steps:
Practice mindfulness: Engage in regular mindfulness practices, such as meditation or prayer, to quiet your mind and become more aware of your thoughts and feelings.
Pay attention to your body: Listen to the signals your body sends you, such as physical sensations, emotions, or energy levels.
These can provide valuable clues about your well-being and guide you in making healthy choices.
Cultivate self-awareness: Develop a deeper understanding of your personal values, beliefs, and desires.
This self-knowledge can help you discern between intuition and other influences, such as fear or wishful thinking.
Create space for reflection: Make time for quiet reflection and contemplation, where you can listen to your inner voice and explore your intuitive insights.

Trust and act on your intuition: When you feel a strong sense of guidance or an intuitive nudge, trust it and take action accordingly.

Pray for discernment: Ask God for the wisdom and discernment to recognize His guidance and the intuition He has placed within you.

Lord Teach Me To	I Am Thankful For

Prayer

Lord, thank You for the gift of intuition and the guidance it provides in my journey towards holistic health. Help me to develop and trust my intuition as I seek to understand my body, mind, and soul's needs.

Grant me the discernment to recognize Your guidance and the courage to follow my inner voice. In Jesus' name, I pray. **Amen.**

Day 35: Overcoming Obstacles and Challenges with Faith

Reflection

In our journey towards holistic health, we may face obstacles and challen-ges that can feel overwhelming or discouraging.
In these moments, it's essential to remember the power of faith and trust in God's plan for our well-being.
By relying on our faith, we can find the strength and resilience to overco-me challenges and continue moving forward on our path to spiritual growth and healing.

Bible Passage : Isaiah 40:29-31 (NIV)

He gives strength to the weary and increases the power of the weak.

Even youths grow tired and weary, and young men stumble and fall;
but those who hope in the Lord will renew their strength.

They will soar on wings like eagles; they will run and not grow weary, they will walk and not be faint.

Application

To overcome obstacles and challenges with faith, consider the following steps:

Acknowledge the challenge: Recognize the difficulty you're facing, and don't try to ignore or downplay it. This honesty allows you to confront the situation head-on and seek the help and support you need.
Turn to God in prayer: Share your concerns, fears, and struggles with God, and ask for His guidance, strength, and wisdom in overcoming the obstacle.
Seek support from others: Reach out to friends, family, or spiritual mentors who can provide encouragement, advice, and prayer support during challenging times.
Focus on the bigger picture: Remind yourself of your ultimate goal of holistic health and the reasons why it's essential to your spiritual journey. This perspective can help you maintain motivation and determination.

Cultivate resilience: Develop mental, emotional, and spiritual resilience by practicing gratitude, meditation, and other spiritual disciplines that help you stay centered and grounded in your faith.

Trust in God's plan: Believe that God is in control and has a purpose for the challenges you face. Trust in His ability to bring about good from even the most difficult situations.

Lord Teach Me To	I Am Thankful For

Prayer

Heavenly Father, I thank You for the strength and resilience that comes from my faith in You. Please help me overcome the obstacles and challenges I encounter on my journey to holistic health.

Remind me to trust in Your plan for my life and to rely on Your guidance and wisdom. Surround me with supportive people who can encourage and uplift me during difficult times. In Jesus' name, I pray. **Amen.**

Day 36: Developing an Attitude of Humility

Reflection

Humility is a vital aspect of holistic health and spiritual growth.

By cultivating an attitude of humility, we can recognize our limitations, remain open to learning, and avoid the pitfalls of pride and ego. Humility allows us to see ourselves and others with compassion and understanding, fostering healthy relationships and promoting spiritual growth.

Bible Passage : Philippians 2:3-5 (NIV)

Do nothing out of selfish ambition or vain conceit. Rather, in humility value others above yourselves, not looking to your own interests but each of you to the interests of the others.

In your relationships with one another, have the same mindset as Christ Jesus.

Application

To develop an attitude of humility, consider the following practices:

Reflect on your strengths and weaknesses: Acknowledge your abilities and achievements, but also recognize your limitations and areas for growth. This self-awareness can help you maintain a balanced perspective of yourself.
Practice active listening: When engaging with others, focus on truly understanding their thoughts, feelings, and experiences. Resist the urge to interrupt or interject with your own opinions and ideas.
Embrace a teachable spirit: Remain open to learning from others and be willing to admit when you're wrong or don't know something. Recognize that everyone has something valuable to teach you.
Serve others: Seek opportunities to help and serve others, both within your community and in your personal relationships. Acts of service can foster humility and remind you of the interconnectedness of all people.

Emulate the example of Jesus: Strive to live with the same mindset and attitude as Jesus, who demonstrated profound humility throughout His life and ministry.

Pray for a humble heart: Regularly ask God to develop humility within you and to reveal any areas where pride or ego may be hindering your spiritual growth.

Lord Teach Me To	**I Am Thankful For**

Prayer

Lord, I ask You to help me cultivate an attitude of humility in my daily life. Teach me to value others above myself, to listen with an open heart, and to be willing to learn from those around me. Guide me in emulating the example of Jesus and in fostering a teachable spirit.
Please reveal any areas of pride or ego that may be hindering my spiritual growth, and grant me the wisdom and grace to overcome them. In Jesus' name, I pray. **Amen.**

Day 37: Cultivating a Heart of Worship and Praise

Reflection

Worship and praise are essential elements of a healthy spiritual life, allowing us to express our gratitude and adoration for God.

By cultivating a heart of worship and praise, we can deepen our connection with God, increase our awareness of His presence in our lives, and maintain a healthy perspective on our own worth and significance.

Bible Passage : Psalm 100:1-5 (NIV)

Shout for joy to the Lord, all the earth.
Worship the Lord with gladness; come before Him with joyful songs.
Know that the Lord is God. It is He who made us, and we are His; we are His people, the sheep of His pasture.
Enter His gates with thanksgiving and His courts with praise; give thanks to Him and praise His name.
For the Lord is good and His love endures forever; His faithfulness continues through all generations.

Application

To cultivate a heart of worship and praise, consider implementing the following practices:
Set aside regular times for worship and praise: Establish a routine for engaging in worship, whether it's through prayer, singing, or meditating on Scripture. This can help you develop a consistent attitude of worship and gratitude.
Recognize God's presence in your daily life: Actively seek out and acknowledge the ways in which God is at work in your life, both in the big moments and the small details.
Express gratitude: Make a habit of thanking God for His blessings, even during difficult or challenging times. This can help you maintain a heart of gratitude and worship.
Use music as a tool for worship: Listen to worship music or hymns that resonate with you, or sing songs of praise to God as a means of expressing your adoration and gratitude.

Engage in corporate worship: Participate in worship services and gatherings with fellow believers, as this can help strengthen your faith and deepen your connection with God.

Reflect on God's attributes: Spend time meditating on the character of God, including His love, mercy, and faithfulness. This can help you grow in your understanding and appreciation of who He is.

Lord Teach Me To	I Am Thankful For

Prayer

Heavenly Father, I ask for Your help in cultivating a heart of worship and praise. Teach me to recognize Your presence in my daily life and to express my gratitude for Your countless blessings.

Guide me in setting aside regular times for worship, and help me to use music, prayer, and meditation as tools for deepening my connection with You. In Jesus' name, I pray. **Amen.**

Day 38: Learning to Let Go and Trust in God's Plan

Reflection

Trusting in God's plan for our lives can be challenging, especially when we face uncertainty or hardship.

However, learning to let go and trust in His plan is essential for maintaining a healthy spiritual life and experiencing the peace and assurance that come from surrendering our worries and concerns to Him.

Bible Passage : Proverbs 3:5-6 (NIV)

Trust in the Lord with all your heart and lean not on your own understanding;

In all your ways submit to Him, and He will make your paths straight.

Application

To learn to let go and trust in God's plan, consider implementing the following practices:

Reflect on past experiences: Consider times in your life when God has guided you or provided for you, even when circumstances seemed uncertain or difficult. This can help you build trust in His faithfulness and provision.

Pray for guidance and wisdom: Regularly seek God's guidance and wisdom in your decision-making and ask for His help in discerning His will for your life.

Surrender your worries and concerns: Actively choose to let go of your worries and concerns, trusting that God is in control and will work all things together for your good.

Embrace uncertainty: Accept that you may not always know what the future holds or understand God's plan for your life, but trust that He is with you and will guide you every step of the way.

Seek support from others: Share your struggles with trusting in God's plan with trusted friends or mentors who can provide encouragement, prayer, and guidance.

Meditate on Scripture: Spend time meditating on Bible verses that speak to God's faithfulness, love, and guidance. This can help you grow in your trust and reliance on Him.

Lord Teach Me To	I Am Thankful For

Prayer

Lord, I confess that it is difficult for me to let go and trust in Your plan for my life. I ask for Your help in surrendering my worries and concerns to You and trusting that You are in control. Grant me the wisdom and discernment to follow Your guidance and to lean on Your understanding rather than my own. Help me to embrace uncertainty and find peace in knowing that You are with me every step of the way. In Jesus' name, I pray. **Amen.**

Day 39: The Power of Spiritual Growth in Healing

Reflection

Trusting in God's plan for our lives can be challenging, especially when we face uncertainty or hardship.

However, learning to let go and trust in His plan is essential for maintaining a healthy spiritual life and experiencing the peace and assurance that come from surrendering our worries and concerns to Him.

Bible Passage : Psalm 103:2-5 (NIV)

Praise the Lord, my soul, and forget not all his benefits—who forgives all your sins and heals all your diseases, who redeems your life from the pit and crowns you with love and compassion, who satisfies your desires with good things so that your youth is renewed like the eagle's.

Application

To experience the power of spiritual growth in healing, consider implementing the following practices:
Regular prayer and meditation: Spend time daily in prayer and meditation, seeking God's guidance and wisdom in your life.
This will help you deepen your connection with Him and draw on His strength in times of need.
Study Scripture: Read and study the Bible regularly to increase your understanding of God's Word and His promises. This can provide you with encouragement and hope during challenging times.
Engage in spiritual disciplines: Participate in spiritual practices, such as fasting, worship, and solitude, to strengthen your spiritual life and foster personal growth.
Seek support from a spiritual community: Surround yourself with a community of believers who can support you in your spiritual journey and offer guidance and encouragement as you grow in your faith.

Practice forgiveness and reconciliation: Embrace the healing power of forgiveness and reconciliation, both with yourself and others, as you seek to grow spiritually and experience healing.

Cultivate an attitude of gratitude: Acknowledge and give thanks for the blessings in your life, even during difficult times. This can help you maintain a positive perspective and promote spiritual growth.

Lord Teach Me To	I Am Thankful For

Prayer

Heavenly Father, I thank You for the opportunity to grow spiritually and experience Your healing power in my life. I pray that You would guide me in my spiritual journey and help me to deepen my connection with You. Strengthen me as I engage in spiritual disciplines and seek support from a spiritual community. Help me to practice forgiveness and cultivate an attitude of gratitude, so I may experience the healing and transformation that come from spiritual growth. In Jesus' name, I pray. **Amen.**

Day 40: Celebrating Your Journey to Holistic Health

Reflection

As you come to the end of these 40 days, it's important to take a moment to celebrate your journey towards holistic health.
You have learned about the different aspects of well-being, including physical, mental, emotional, and spiritual health, and have taken steps to nurture each of these areas in your life.

As you continue on your journey, remember that holistic health is an ongoing process, and there will always be room for growth and improvement.
Celebrate your progress, be patient with yourself, and continue to seek God's guidance and strength as you strive for a life of balance, well-being, and fulfillment.

Bible Passage : Philippians 4:4-9 (NIV)

Rejoice in the Lord always. I will say it again: Rejoice!
Let your gentleness be evident to all. The Lord is near.
Do not be anxious about anything, but in every situation, by prayer and petition, with thanksgiving, present your requests to God.

And the peace of God, which transcends all understanding, will guard your hearts and your minds in Christ Jesus. Finally, brothers and sisters, whatever is true, whatever is noble, whatever is right, whatever is pure, whatever is lovely, whatever is admirable—if anything is excellent or praiseworthy—think about such things.

Whatever you have learned or received or heard from me, or seen in me—put it into practice. And the God of peace will be with you.

Application

As you celebrate your journey to holistic health, consider the following:

Reflect on the progress you've made and the positive changes you've experienced in your life over the past 40 days.

Take time to express gratitude to God for His guidance and support throughout your journey.

Share your experiences and insights with others, offering encouragement and support as they embark on their own journey towards holistic health.

Continue to engage in the practices and disciplines you've learned, making them a consistent part of your daily routine.

Remain open to growth and change, seeking new opportunities for personal and spiritual development.

Lord Teach Me To

I Am Thankful For

Prayer

Gracious God, I thank You for guiding me on this journey towards holistic health. I celebrate the progress I've made and the positive changes I've experienced in my life. Help me to continue growing in my understanding of Your love and the importance of nurturing my body, mind, and soul. As I move forward, please continue to guide me in my pursuit of balance, well-being, and fulfillment. May I be a source of encouragement and support for others on their journey, sharing Your love and grace with all those I meet. In Jesus' name, I pray.**Amen.**

Week 1: The Foundation of Holistic Health

Weekly Reflection

As you reflect on the first week of your journey, consider the key concepts and principles you've learned about holistic health.

What does it mean to view health in a holistic way, and how does this perspective differ from a more traditional approach to wellness?

How has your understanding of the connection between your body, mind, and soul deepened over the past week?

What steps have you taken to begin nurturing each of these aspects of your well-being?

Journal Prompt

Write about a moment during the past week when you felt a strong sense of connection between your body, mind, and soul.

Describe the experience and how it impacted your understanding of holistic health.

Week 2: Nurturing Your Body, Mind, and Soul

Weekly Reflection

Reflection: In the second week of your journey, you've explored various practices and disciplines designed to nurture your physical, mental, and spiritual health.

As you reflect on the past week, consider the new habits and routines you've adopted and the impact they've had on your overall well-being. How have these practices contributed to your sense of balance and wholeness?

What challenges or obstacles have you encountered in implementing these practices, and how have you worked to overcome them?

Journal Prompt

Choose one new habit or practice you've implemented during the past week, and write about the impact it has had on your well-being.

What have you learned from this practice, and how do you plan to continue incorporating it into your daily routine?

Week 3: Embracing the Power of Prayer, Meditation, and Mindfulness

Weekly Reflection

During the third week of your journey, you've delved deeper into the power of prayer, meditation, and mindfulness as key components of holistic health.

Reflect on the ways in which these practices have enhanced your spiritual growth, mental clarity, and emotional well-being. Have you experienced any shifts in your perspective or attitude as a result of incorporating prayer, meditation, and mindfulness into your daily routine?

What insights or revelations have emerged from your practice of these disciplines?

Journal Prompt

Write about a specific insight or revelation you've gained through your practice of prayer, meditation, or mindfulness.

How has this insight impacted your overall approach to holistic health and well-being?

Week 4: Cultivating Positive Relationships and Community

Weekly Reflection

As you reflect on the fourth week of your journey, consider the role of relationships and community in your pursuit of holistic health.

How have you worked to build strong, supportive connections with others during this time?

What steps have you taken to invest in your relationships and to create a sense of belonging and community?

How have these efforts contributed to your overall sense of well-being and fulfillment?

Journal Prompt

Describe a meaningful interaction or connection you've made during the past week, and write about how this connection has contributed to your pursuit of holistic health.

What steps can you take to continue nurturing this relationship and fostering a sense of community?

Week 5: Overcoming Challenges and Embracing Growth
Weekly Reflection

Reflection: In the fifth week of your journey, you've faced various challenges and obstacles on your path to holistic health.
As you reflect on this past week, consider the ways in which you've worked to overcome these challenges and the lessons you've learned in the process.

How has your faith and trust in God's guidance and support grown during this time?

In what ways have you embraced personal growth and change, and how has this contributed to your journey towards holistic health?

Journal Prompt

Write about a specific challenge or obstacle you've faced during the past week, and describe the steps you've taken to overcome it.

What lessons have you learned from this experience, and how will you apply these lessons as you continue on your journey towards holistic health?

Week 6: Celebrating Your Journey to Holistic Health Weekly Reflection

As you reach the end of your 40-day journey, take time to reflect on the progress you've made and the growth you've experienced in your pursuit of holistic health.

Consider the various aspects of your well-being - physical, mental, emotional, and spiritual - and the ways in which your understanding and practice of holistic health have evolved over the past six weeks.

What are some of the most significant milestones or breakthroughs you've achieved during this time?

How have your relationships, sense of purpose, and connection to God deepened as a result of your commitment to holistic health?

Journal Prompt

Write a letter to yourself, reflecting on the progress you've made and the growth you've experienced during your 40-day journey to holistic health.

Offer words of encouragement, gratitude, and wisdom to help guide you as you continue on your path to greater well-being and fulfillment.

Day : ______

Reflection

Bible Passage : ______

Application

Lord Teach Me To

I Am Thankful For

Prayer

Day :

Reflection

Bible Passage :

Application

Lord Teach Me To

I Am Thankful For

Prayer

Day :

Reflection

Bible Passage :

Application

Lord Teach Me To

I Am Thankful For

Prayer

Day : ______________________

Reflection

Bible Passage : ______________________

Application

Lord Teach Me To

I Am Thankful For

Prayer

Day :

Reflection

Bible Passage :

Application

Lord Teach Me To

I Am Thankful For

Prayer

Day : ______________________

Reflection

Bible Passage : ______________________

Application

Lord Teach Me To

I Am Thankful For

Prayer

Day : ____________________

Reflection

Bible Passage : ____________________

Application

Lord Teach Me To

I Am Thankful For

Prayer

Day : ______________________

Reflection

Bible Passage : ______________________

Application

Lord Teach Me To

I Am Thankful For

Prayer

Day :

Reflection

Bible Passage :

Application

Lord Teach Me To

I Am Thankful For

Prayer

Day : ______________________

Reflection

Bible Passage : ______________________

Application

Lord Teach Me To

I Am Thankful For

Prayer

Day : ____________________

Reflection

Bible Passage : ____________________

Application

Lord Teach Me To

I Am Thankful For

Prayer

Conclusion

As we come to the end of our 40-day journey to holistic health, it's essential to take a moment to reflect on the progress we've made and the lessons we've learned. Throughout this transformative experience, we've delved into various aspects of our well-being, including physical, mental, emotional, and spiritual health. By integrating these components, we've begun to understand the interconnected nature of our existence and the importance of nurturing our whole selves.

Over the past 40 days, we've explored topics such as proper nutrition, physical activity, stress management, mental clarity, prayer, meditation, gratitude, sleep habits, relationships, self-care, forgiveness, and spiritual growth, among others. Each day has brought new insights and opportunities for personal reflection and growth, equipping us with the knowledge and tools to lead more balanced, fulfilling lives.

As we conclude this journey, it's important to remember that the path to holistic health is not a destination but a continuous process. The habits and practices we've cultivated during these 40 days are merely the beginning of a lifelong commitment to nurturing our body, mind, and soul. We must remain diligent in our efforts to maintain and build upon the progress we've made, and we must never underestimate the power of small, consistent steps toward greater health and happiness.

In the pursuit of holistic health, we must also remember to extend grace and compassion to ourselves. Our journey will inevitably be marked by setbacks, challenges, and moments of doubt, but these experiences are a natural part of growth and transformation. Embrace these moments as opportunities for learning and self-discovery, trusting that each step, whether it is forward or backward, contributes to the larger tapestry of your journey.

Lastly, let us not forget the essential role of faith and our connection to the Divine in our quest for holistic health. As we continue to deepen our relationship with God, we will find greater peace, strength, and wisdom to navigate life's complexities. Our spiritual foundation provides a source of unshakable support and guidance, even in the most challenging of times.

As we move forward from these 40 days, may we carry with us the lessons and insights we've gained, embracing each day as an opportunity to grow and evolve in our pursuit of holistic health. May we be ever mindful of the interconnected nature of our existence, honoring our body, mind, and soul as sacred vessels of the Divine. And may we continue to seek the wisdom, guidance, and support of our Creator as we journey toward greater well-being, happiness, and fulfillment.

Thank you for joining me on this journey, and may the blessings of holistic health, love, and grace abound in your life now and always.

With gratitude and hope,

Faith Shepherd

Faith Shepherd's books offer a powerful and inspiring message of hope, faith, and love. Her books are perfect for those seeking to deepen their spiritual journey and grow in their relationship with God.
Through her insightful and thought-provoking writing, **Faith Shepherd** shares practical wisdom and guidance for living a more purposeful and fulfilling life.

If you're looking for uplifting and inspiring reading material, don't hesitate to check out Faith Shepherd's books!

Made in the USA
Monee, IL
21 November 2023